Table of Contents

Preface

I remember sitting outside a closed business around two or three in the morning, with my legs close to my chest and arms wrapped around them. The tears rolled down my cheeks, hoping he would not find me. I would pray, "Not today."

In the distance, I could hear his truck roaring down the street. So, I'd move from building to building in the dark, praying "Not today." When the sound muffled, I knew he was heading away from me and I could breathe. I'd think, "Maybe not this time." My biggest fear would be, will he point a gun to my head telling me to beg for my life once again, or will he end it this time?

I waited that day for him to finally go to sleep before going home. I thought, then when he wakes up, he will not be angry. He might be mad all day but eventually, I will cook him breakfast, then lunch and dinner, and try to get back on his good side, all the while, asking God why me? Why does the

ISBN: Paperback 978-1-64873-145-7
ISNB: EBOOK 978-1-64873-301-7

Printed in the United States of America

Published by:
Writer's Publishing House
Prescott, Az 86301

Cover Design: Creative Artistic Excellence

Project Management and Book Launch by Creative Artistic Excellence Marketing https://lizzymcnett.com

A Business Called Life

By Maria Sanchez-Bueno

person who is supposed to protect and take care of me because I married him treat me this way?

I graduated in 2001 from Skyline High School. My life had always been filled with love and respect. I went to school and never got into any arguments. As a child, I never gave my parents problems. Even during my childhood, I helped take care of my three younger siblings. My frustration was not directed at God, rather I was confused as to why this was happening to me. What did I do wrong to have found someone like him? What was I doing wrong in my relationship to keep having the same effect? What could I do to make it better?

As time passed, through trial and error I made some changes without thinking. The lessons taught me if I can help family or friends, or even someone who buys *A Business Called Life*, it will show the purpose of my life experiences. The question I have always asked God have been answered: Why me? No matter what has happened He has been beside me every step of the way. It's up to the individual whether we see it or not.

A Business Called Life encourages people to make wise life decisions. My goal is to express other options to clear a path that may better suit them in the future. Just as I had done, at that moment.

I look at my life now and have learned that everything we do in life is a result of our actions; it's has a cause and effect. Life should be treated as a business; how you raise your children or handle business affairs, the same method applies to marriage or relationships. I mean every aspect of life: health, toxic associations, everything!

The better business decisions we make throughout life can have a tremendous impact on everyone around us. Or, simply giving someone encouragement can create life-altering effects. We can do better by applying some simple practices as we progress through life.

Introduction

"You will meet two kinds of people in life: ones who build you up and ones who tear you down. But in the end, you'll thank them both." - Unknown

My career in real estate started over eleven years ago. Over time, I have worked with some of the best-known brokers in the country, including Keller Williams, Coldwell Banker, Century 21, and currently with RE/MAX Town & Country. As an agent, my job is to "match" families with their first home, or help people find their dream homes. I also help many others seeking to downsize or upgrade. One of my favorite aspects of my job is the relationships I have built along the way. In these connections, both parties walked away with increased knowledge.

As you read in the preface, my first marriage did not last, but I am hoping the second one will be everlasting. My method of making decisions in life as a business did not apply when I met my current husband, it came later. I was lucky enough to meet someone that feels the same as I do: "Treat each other as you want to be treated."

It was a mutual understanding that we treat our marriage as a business. We are two CEOs combining a business called marriage. Everything we do as an individual or couple affects both of us. One of the biggest investments we have together is our children: our fourteen-year-old son Angel, and ten-year-old daughter Emily. They motivate us to be a better couple, better parents, better aunts, and uncles, and overall, better humans for a better society.

The experience of my first marriage taught me a lot when looking for my next partner in life, including what to stay away from, and what I can accept as a wife and from a husband. I am thankful for my first marriage because it has made my second marriage stronger. We have grown together to become much stronger, more affluent individuals. Hence the reason for writing this book.

The contents of this book were created to show why it is important for any relationship to be treated as a business. As an example, Emily my daughter, I want her to learn from my mistakes. Then she can take my experiences and understand it is not alright for a husband to humiliate his wife. On the other hand, Angel must learn to treat a woman like a lady. To love and respect one another mutually. In these examples, they can learn to treat any relationship like a business.

One example that you will read about in the book is the art of 'Interviewing.' Yes, the only way to truly understand someone is by having a heart-deep conversation. In this interaction, you can learn what the other person can bring to the table. A relationship grows with a side-by-side, win-win mentality, as my broker Michael Coburn says about our clients.

As I have evolved into a better realtor, my experiences have been applied to my everyday life. Michael Coburn has taught us to use the win-win mentality when listing a home for sale. In other words, if the seller wins then the agents win. Both sides of the transaction should win to be happy.

Several years ago, I began perfecting this frame of mind and created a foundation with which anyone can learn to treat their life as a business. If I invest in my children (this doesn't always mean money) by spending time with them, talking to them about their future, and pushing them towards those ideals, we feel as a team that everyone wins. The same action applies to health: invest at least thirty minutes a day in exercise and it will be a win-win situation. Maybe, you can shave off a chronic illness, like diabetes or heart disease. The choice is solely up to you.

On another note, when looking at relationships with friends, can you honestly say, you are in a win-win relationship with them? Or is it only one side winning? If so, maybe it's time to adjust and let go.

Chapter One:

Letting Go

"Letting go means to realize that some people are a part of your history, but not a part of your destiny."-
Steve Maraboli

T he day I left was a hot summer day in Texas. My husband and myself had been invited to a party with friends and family. It started as one of those days that had left an uneasy feeling in my stomach wondering if I should even go with him to the party or not go at all. In the past, most parties we attended always ended in a fight. I had concluded that it was better for us to not go out anymore to avoid fighting. He would either drink too much or think that I was flirting with someone. Then the argument continued over him giving me the keys to drive because he was drunk, however, that day was different. It had been a while since we went out and I thought maybe we should try one more time. That day the weather was bad and raining pretty steadily. Although, I ignored my uncertainty and I agreed to go along, plus my son's God-parents were going to be there and it usually meant he drank less.

As the day progressed, he drank not excessively but too much to drive home safely. We had agreed that I would drive us home if he wanted to drink. I was ok with him drinking as long as he was not driving. My son was thirteen months old and the last thing I wanted was to ride home with a drunk driver. There had been several other instances where he almost lost control of the truck driving while intoxicated. A couple of weeks before we moved in together, he was in a car accident where he had flipped and totaled his car. But now, instead of just us, I had to consider my child's safety. He was the one person I loved the most, and as a parent, he was my responsibility. As usual, my husband did not consider our safety when he had been drinking.

My stress level rose when it was time to leave, but since I had the keys that day, I assumed the problem would be avoided. He walked up to the truck and put the car seat in the backseat while I went over to the driver's side.

Of course, he took the keys from my hand, and said, "I'm driving as always."

The reception hall had large full-length windows and they were all open. So, the guests could see us by the truck. I went around as if I was getting in the passenger side but instead as quick as I could I got Angel out of the car seat and walked as fast as I could back to the reception. The last thing I wanted was to fight about the keys, in front of all the guests. Yet, getting in the truck with him driving terrified me.

"Just stop acting like a bitch and get in…." he said quietly.

We both remained calm, so no one was the wiser.

"No… not with my son in the truck. Please let me drive?"

At that moment, fate took control. My son's God-parents approached and asked if everything was alright.

"Yes, thank you… Joe has to go pick up his son and I didn't want to go. (Joe had a son from a previous relationship.) Would you mind giving me and the baby a ride home?"

"Of course, we would be happy to give you a ride."

We live close by so it didn't take them out of their way. Plus, one of their daughters was ready to go home as well and she also offered to take Angel and me home. We arrived home a few minutes later and I thanked her for the ride. I headed to the door with my son in my arms. We were living with my husband's mom and stepdad at the time and their house was very secluded. It was surrounded by trees covering much of the house and a long driveway. The house had several large steps leading to the front door. Angel and I were halfway down the long driveway which headed to the house when I heard someone running up from behind me. I turned and saw Joe chasing me. In a panic, I ran but carrying Angel there was no way to outrun him. He caught me before I could get close to the steps that led up to the house. Needless to say, he grabbed me by the back of the head; my hair was almost waist length which he also wrapped around his wrist. After he got control of me, he put both hands on the side of my head and pulled me over by the trailer he had been using for our moving business. Then he started slamming my head against the side of the trailer.

My son started crying. "Stop, please let me put Angel down. You can keep hitting me just let me put him down first!" It did not matter, he kept hitting me.

A few minutes later, his mother and stepdad heard the commotion and stepped outside. He ignored their approach and continued the assault until his stepdad was able to get me loose. His mom kept yelling, "Stop, Joe! Go take Angel upstairs," she told me.

I ran and managed to get up three steps before he grabbed my hair once again and threw me on the ground, while I was still holding the baby. When his mom caught up, he let me go.

Angel was screaming by this time; I was fighting to keep ahold of him since the patio was concrete and I didn't want to drop him. I did manage to get inside with help from his mother.

"You need to leave my house," she told him. This was not the first time she had seen her son abuse his wife or girlfriend. "Call the police and don't let him treat you like that," she advised me.

I loved his mom, and she helped me tremendously. As a matter of fact, she helped me get my cosmetology license, so I could get a better job and work for her in the salon she owned. She had done so much for us and I felt her pain. I would not want my son to go to jail or prison. His mom would suffer the consequences for years, and so I did not want to be the one to send him back for a longer time. My first instinct at that time was to think of others before myself.

Once the dust settled somewhat, I called my dad and brother to come pick me up, the last thing I wanted was to leave and be alone. I did not have a car of my own at the time. I worked hard to help my husband pay the bills but he would not allow me to buy a car. He would say why spend money on a car when we have bills to pay plus, he was letting me use his car. He, however, had recently purchased a new truck.

It took my dad and brother about ten minutes to arrive. My dad was holding Angel in the living room, while my brother came to help me stuff my things into trash bags.

Then, in this midst of packing, Joe stormed in and said with audacity, "Are you really leaving? You are just making a big deal out of nothing. Besides, this is your fault for making a fool out of me at the party. You always know how to push my buttons."

I am sure I am not the only one who has heard those words before. "You know how to push my buttons" are words to make us feel we are to blame for their actions against us, the victims.

If I learned anything, it was things would only continue to get worse each time I went back. I continued to pack quickly, as I was worried, he might hurt my brother. He always threatened to hurt my brothers if they ever got in his way. So, I packed as fast as I could because the only thing that mattered was my and Angel's clothing. My jewelry, pictures, high school diploma, and memorabilia, everything else didn't matter. Everything else could stay behind, and so it did.

My only concern was for my son; I didn't care what happened to me. The experience taught me two things: the first being if I stayed my son might turn out like his dad, or he would learn this is normal behavior and end up abusing his wife or girlfriends, like his dad. The second reason was, if we stayed, Angel might grow up to hate his father. Either way, Angel would lose.

I had to make the decision quickly since I wanted a better life for both of us. My heart was beating faster, my palms were sweaty, I was scared and I wanted to cry all at once. At that point, the only option was to leave. While packing, there was a struggle in my head. Many emotions were running through my body, thoughts of leaving, and others of staying. But then the love I had for my son overpowered everything else. I packed all those emotions in the trash bags with our clothes while I filled my head with courage and faith. So, I made the best decision of my life and WE left.

Self-Reflection

What emotions am I struggling with that could have a major impact on my life?

_____

_____

_____

Am I in a bad relationship that I am struggling to walk away from?

_____

_____

_____

Why am I staying?

_____

_____

_____

How can my life improve by leaving the
relationship?

_____

_____

_____

What steps can I take to leave sooner rather than
later?

_____

_____

_____

Chapter Two:

The Grass Is Not Always Greener on The Other Side

"She is his heart… He is her armor." -Unknown

I was twenty, naïve, and in love with a man three years older than me, and this is how my story began. One afternoon I got into an argument with my parents and Joe convinced me to leave, telling me that the rest of my life would always be the same thing if I stayed living with them. Regardless, his reality and the truth were two different forecasts.

It was not a bad life living with my parents, however, being the oldest I was tired of being everyone's mother. Since I was a teenager, it was expected that I help take care of my younger siblings. I was responsible for things like homework, watching them play outside, cleaning the house and starting to cook dinner if my parents were delayed at work. The tradition was not just in my household, it was typical for the Hispanic community. In most cases our parents cannot afford to pay a babysitter, so instead, the oldest has to take that responsibility whether we agree or not. Therefore, I couldn't join any after school activities, as I had to go home and make sure my siblings were safe. At my age, I couldn't leave without asking permission. They insisted on knowing my whereabouts at all times.

On that fateful day, we had an argument over my brothers not helping around the house which left all the responsibility on me. I had already graduated high school and was working in a medical clinic but still had the responsibility of my siblings, because both my parents worked and I got home before them. Most of the time the house was cleaned and I had already cooked by the time my parents got home.

The day after the argument with my parents, I walked to my boyfriend's house. It took me about thirty minutes to get there and I was happy to see him. I was venting to him about the argument; how I thought it was unfair. Of course, he was very understanding and asked me to move in with him.

"I am almost twenty-one and can do whatever I want," I thought. At that time, I thought, "Well, I already work, cook, clean, and help my brothers and sister. It will be a piece of cake to only take care of him and myself. We can stay out as late as we want and only worry about ourselves and nothing else." I instantly fell in love with the proposition; it was the best thing he could have ever said to me.

"Alright, you are right. I am ready to move." My life would always be the same with my parents and something had to change.

My dad's birthday was that day, which is also a day before mine, but since he was tired from work, we weren't doing anything to celebrate. When I arrived back home, I walked in the front door and went straight to my room, and packed two small suitcases. Then I went back into the living room and my dad was sitting in his favorite chair.

I informed him, "I have helped you a lot and it's time for you to see all I have done for everyone around here, so I think it's time for me to leave." The tears rolled down my cheeks.

He looked straight at me. "Do what you think is best for yourself, you're already an adult and I cannot stop you from making the decision you want to make."

His reaction surprised me in a way, I guess. Inside, I wanted him to try and stop me and say something to make me stay. I wanted him to tell me things would change, and he would make my brothers help me. Or something along those lines.

Among my siblings, I was closest to my dad, and because of my age we were able to talk about almost anything. In a way, a piece of my heart broke that night. I was leaving him behind. Not to mention, my little sister, whom I had raised since she was born. My chores included changing diapers, bathing, feeding, and doing her hair. Then, as she got older, I helped her get to school and do her homework. Many times, I even went to parent conferences because my parents were working and couldn't attend. She in many ways was like my daughter, but I thought that it should have been my time to take care of myself. I thought the grass was greener on the other side, so I grabbed my things and walked out the door.

About a week later, I started to feel melancholy. The depression kicked in but I had no idea why. This was supposed to be a happy time, a joyous period to enjoy my new life. Before long, the sorrow became unbearable. I missed my family, the house, my room. I started to cry at night and Joe began to worry about me, or so I thought.

"What's wrong?" Joe asked.

"I miss my family, and I'm regretting leaving." I sobbed through our conversation.

The last thing I wanted was for his parents to hear me crying. Then the reality of my decision hit hard: Joe jumped out of bed and started yelling at me. "You are a grown-ass woman and you have nothing to cry about. If you want to go back to the same life, then go ahead. Pack your shit and leave."

It was obvious to me I had made a bad decision, so I got up and started packing my things. When I was about half-way done packing, he grabbed my luggage and threw everything outside. "If you want to leave, you'll go with nothing. You are not taking anything from this house. I'll burn all of it before you take anything."

"Okay," I told him.

I was determined to leave so much more now after seeing his reaction. I took my purse and headed out of the bedroom, but he grabbed my arm and threw me on the bed. He took the phone cord and used it to tie up my hands and feet behind my back. I was face down on the bed, crying begging him to stop.

"Why are you doing this?" It was the last thing I expected to happen, especially from the man I loved.

A few minutes later, we both calmed down. He untied me and we sat on the floor and talked. He convinced me I was grown and there was no reason to be crying for my family. In what I thought was love, his words made sense; *maybe I was overreacting*...

Then under the circumstances, the last thing I wanted was going back to the same problems, and at the time I had no idea if they would even forgive me. I had already left with a man and was scared my parents wouldn't accept me back. In my mind, it was best to suck it up and stay. The conversation was followed by declarations of love and he never wanted me to leave him. I was in love with him and didn't know how to react. I didn't know if that's how relationships were once you were living together and with him being so apologetic to me, I thought it wouldn't happen again.

Joe was very good at manipulating the situation, he had completely convinced me I was better off with him, and my parents would never change, nor take me back. Of course, they had no idea of the danger I was in at the time.

As the night progress, we started talking more and laughing; it was like when we first met. "Please forgive me, Maria…. Will you marry me?"

I thought it was the best thing that could have ever happened. "Yes, I will marry you."

We got married by common law. I had a protector, a husband who would take care of me the way I would take care of him. He would love me with his heart and guard me with his shield.

We agreed to save money and work on getting our own house; it would give us a fresh start. I imagined my parents would be happy to know I was getting married and he would provide me with a home.

We had a small wedding with the Justice of the Peace at his mom's house; we invited our close family and some friends. I was happy thinking all my problems were gone because we were in love. For the next couple of months, we rented a small house the same distance between my parents and his mom's. It was great for a couple of months. I maintained my regular job working as a medical assistant while attending cosmetology school and Joe stayed steadily employed. We had a small two-bedroom house and we arranged one room for his then six-year-old son who spent time with us on the weekends.

Before long the arguments started again, but not as severe. He would push or pull me and call me names but, in my mind, it was not that bad. We were married and it was for better or for worse, I didn't want to leave. We were married and would have to adjust. Things should get better.

It turns out things didn't get better, they got worse. The arguments grew more violent; then he started abusing me so that the bruises could not be seen by other people. My visits home to my parents became less and less, more out of fear of them seeing the bruises (these are some signs that parents should be aware of). The last thing I wanted to do was admit my marriage failed, so I didn't tell anyone, except my best friend since high school, Remijio Urena, who had become like my brother from another mother.

Joe had also become friends with my best friend and I felt he was the only one who could talk some sense into him. Every time we would get into an altercation where I feared the worse, I would manage to call Mijio (short for Remijio). He would stop by our house casually with a six-pack of beers and act as if he was just visiting until Joe was calm and no longer mad at me. I don't know if it's a man thing but Mijio always had the right words to say to him while looking out for my best interests. He was the only person I could call and I knew would be there to help.

After one of the fights, we had one day, I walked out of the house hoping Joe would calm down. But instead, he caught me about a block away. "Get in!" he screamed.

"I am going to my parents' house, so he can calm down. I won't tell anyone and will come back when

Joe calms down. I just need to take a walk," I thought.

Some guys were sitting on their front porch witnessing the yelling and me demanding him to leave me alone. Then the incident suddenly got worse: he got out of the car with his pistol and headed toward the people on the porch. "Come on.... I'll get in the car. Just don't hurt anyone," I said.

He drove to an empty lot surrounded by trees and branches and pulled me out of the car. He dragged me through the vacant field, saying, "You know if I kill you and bury you here no one will ever find you?" Once we were in the open field, he forced me to kneel and pointed the gun at the back of my head. "Come on.... now beg for your life."

It was now the third time he had made me beg for my life with a gun pointed at my head. By this time, I said, "I don't want to die but you do what you must."

I was exhausted and had lost all hope. His threatening me with a gun had become routine. Each time I asked, "God why my husband, my protector, the person who is supposed to love me and take care of me? Why is he treating me this way?"

The whole scene left me broken; there were no answers and I started to wonder what I was doing wrong. I didn't know what to do.

By the time I turned twenty-four, I had my cosmetology license, was working two jobs, and gave birth to our son Angel. We had decided to move in with his mom after we found out we were pregnant. We thought it would be a good idea to move back with her and save money for the baby. I was happy again, thinking Joe was going to change. We had a little one to protect; it seemed obvious with Angel he would become a better person. This worked for a few months, and there were no major fights. At least, threatening my life stopped during my pregnancy.

Angel was born in April 2006. It was Good Friday and we were released from the hospital on Easter Sunday. I took this as a sign, a good sign. I was no longer by myself. I fell in love with Angel as soon as I laid eyes on him. He was mine; I was his, and that made me happy. It was the purest love I had ever felt.

Needless to say, the fights began again, and I fell into severe depression. Joe's indifference toward Angel started to bother me.

For the next part, I must protect my son's feelings, so I will not go into detail. He would get jealous of the love I showed for Angel and that made him very angry at times. But this helped me create a stronger bond with Angel.

My son was my world. I finally had someone to love unconditionally and knew he would love me the same way. I now had someone to care for, love, and protect the way I had expected my husband to do for me and sadly fell short of accomplishing.

Self-Reflection

I realized that even though I hoped Joe would change with the arrival of our son, he wasn't going to change. He already had one son and he hadn't changed for him, so why did I expect it to be different with my son? People don't need any excuse to change, it must come from within to make that change. Many people marry the wrong person thinking we can change them. However, if we treated them as a business from the beginning, many problems could be avoided.

How can I learn to treat my relationship like a business?

_____

_____

_____

How can I change to help me avoid these toxic
people in the future?

_____

_____

_____

What can I do to avoid marrying someone who is
not compatible again?

_____

_____

_____

How will this new relationship affect my children?

_____

_____

_____

Chapter Three:

New Beginnings

"For I know the plans I have for you', declares the Lord, 'plans to prosper you and not to harm you, plans to give you hope and a future'." -Jeremiah 29:11

I must admit the first few weeks after we left was very difficult, and mentally draining. My thoughts kept focusing on whether I made the right decision. Humans get used to a certain environment and when they move, it takes time to adjust. It does not matter if the situation is good or bad, the body does not know the difference. In this case, my concerns were over whether I had made the right decision for my son, Angel. I wanted to give him the world and more but was doubting if not having his father around was a good thing for him. One fond memory I have was singing Angel a song called "Yo te esperaba" by Mexican artist Alejandra Guzman. The song talks about her as a pregnant mother and waiting for the arrival of her unborn child.

In the lyrics, she describes how it felt when her baby moved inside her as she counted down the days of the arrival on the calendar. She imagined the color of the baby's eyes and voice tone while thinking of a name she would eventually give the baby. The song goes on to say, she had never been happier and she begged that her baby would thrive one day; on top of the world and be more successful than she was. As the world is unchangeable, she promised to always be there and hold their hand. I would sing that song to Angel all the time, and to this day we sing it together whenever we hear it somewhere.

The lyrics had meaning to me. I wanted to give Angel the best in life but was afraid of losing an opportunity to be with his father.

Thank goodness I stuck with my instincts and stayed living with my parents while allowing Joe to visit. I did not force child support, as I witnessed first-hand how he treated his oldest son when he stayed with us. The last thing I wanted was Joe telling Angel the same things he told his son about having to pay child support. I intended to protect my son whenever possible. Including the two times, Joe came to visit, shortly thereafter he stopped asking to see his son. As I look back now, it was a blessing Angel was only fourteen months old, and had not developed a bond. Besides, Joe usually found some excuse not to take care of him when we were together, and babies for the most part sleep a lot, so bonding is less at that time. Joe did not understand the connection is developed over time. The last time he came to visit, Angel did not want to be with him and started crying, so he got disgusted and handed him back.

My parents and sister, Miriam, were a blessing during those years. As a single parent, I continued to work at my mother-in-law's salon (I had not filed for divorce, yet). I still needed her help and she wanted to do as much as possible, however, the hours were extreme. I worked from 10 to 8:30, five days a week, which limited my time with Angel. It was important to me that he understood I would always be there for him, even if his father was not around. Therefore, I needed to find a career that allowed me to be home more with my son. At the time, my option was real estate. So, I started taking online classes at home.

It took me some time to adjust, as I was not a salesperson. I always considered myself an introvert and hated talking on the phone, but my situation forced me to overcome my fears. The classes and studying took me almost ten months, and then I had to pass the state exam. I would go home from work, eat dinner, spend time with Angel and my family, put Angel to sleep, and put as many hours as I could into my on-line course.

At times when you think you can't do something, just do what Dory did: "Just keep swimming. Just keep swimming."

On the day of my test, I was very nervous, but I had to take the Texas state exam. When the results came back, I failed by 3 points and it devastated me. Nevertheless, the last thing I was going to do was give up. The idea of throwing away my hard work, sweat, and tears did not sit well. So, it was back to the grindstone. I reviewed everything a few more times and rescheduled the test. A few days later, I took the test again and passed. I felt relieved!! It gave me a sense of relief knowing I could provide a better life for us. I was thankful to my family for all their help and support. Our future looked much brighter, with help from God and my faith to believe in His blessings.

It's impossible to know God's plan for our lives, you just have to keep pushing forward doing the best you can. If we go along for the ride and have faith, everything will work out just fine.

Once the test was over and I had something to look forward to I filed for divorce. My heart was ready to feel loved by someone deserving and respectful of us. Although I did not feel attractive, I kept hoping. There were positive male role models in my life, starting with my dad, Jorge, and grandpa,

Cirilo. Since they are good men, I knew there were others in the world.

It was time, and after my divorce, I got back into the dating scene. My dating method was like everyone else and assumed Mr. Right would just come along and sweep me off my feet. So, when I found someone I liked, I dated him. We had no discussions or questions and I learned as we went along. The idea of interviewing someone before we dated was not something I considered. I didn't apply the techniques that you will learn in this book.

It takes a proper mindset to change the way you look at life, along with dating and your career. At the time, I was not aware of these techniques and wasted time dating men that were not a good match. My career, parenting, marriage, and the twelve years after the divorce taught me the proper mindset for success in any endeavor.

After a couple of failures, I started dating my current husband, Octavio, whom I had originally met in high school. We both attended Skyline High

School and we met through a mutual friend. He was cute, with colored eyes, smart, friendly, and in shape. But at that time, I was not interested. We were just friends. He was a smarty pants and I honestly was not attracted to someone smarter than me. I had advanced classes and was considered smart, but most girls in high school are not looking for a guy smarter than them. I was interested in more of the "bad boy." My interest showed me just what bad meant.

I graduated in 2001, a year before Octavio, and we lost communication. We reconnected later on at the beauty salon before I quit. He knew I was married with a child, and when I told him we were divorced, he asked me out. I turned him down several times because he was friends with my ex-brother-in-law. At the time, I was not aware they had gone their separate ways after high school and were no longer close friends.

He visited every Sunday for a haircut and sometimes brought his nephew, Jr. I was impressed by how well he treated his nephew and loved the respect he showed him at the same time. Jr. was eight and no matter what happened, he was kind, stern, but always loving. They were cute amid the men trying to show their macho side in the salon (was more of a barbershop).

One day, Octavio came in as always and wanted to know if I had plans after work. We closed at 6:00 on Sundays so I said, "I am taking my son and sister to church. Would you like to come along?" I never really invited anyone to church but it felt right. Anyway, I assumed he would say no.

"Thank you, I would like to come along." I was surprised.

He passed along his phone number and asked me to call him when I was ready to leave. I am not sure if it was in the cards or not, but I ended up losing the note. Lucky for me, his number was so easy that I memorized it within the few times I had looked at it.

I called him when we were almost ready to leave and he replied, "My cousin asked me to help him put in this new stereo and it took longer than expected, I have to cancel. Can I make it up to you another day?" I agreed to the invite.

I mentioned the date to one of my coworkers and she seemed excited for me. Everybody at the shop knew of my past and wanted me to be happy. They all thought Octavio was kind, respectful, and caring, although I still had my doubts. I didn't know if it was the right time for me and if he was the right person for me to see.

A couple of days later Octavio called to invite me to dinner. I agreed and he picked me up and took me to Olive Garden. When we sat down to order, I was concerned about whether or not he would order an alcoholic drink, but when he stated he did not drink I admired that about him. We talked about my past, but mostly I listened to him tell me his story. However, keep in mind I had no idea what kind of questions to ask. Instead, I just looked into his pretty eyes, assuming he was being honest. We did know each other in high school, so I would have known if he lied.

After our dinner conversation, it occurred to me that he was much like my dad. The way he talked about his mom, nephew, and niece made me feel like he was a family guy. I liked that about him. We continued to date, but as I feared, my ex-husband found out and he started to threaten me again. The stalking began, then the phone calls telling me to break it off or he'd kill both of us. Of course, I feared for Octavio's safety so I broke it off. My next step was filing for a restraining order.

Octavio was very kind. "I can take care of you. We could take care of each other. You are a good person; I want to continue getting to know you." To him, I was "worth the risk" and nothing, or no one would scare him away. I was flattered but scared to see him get hurt. I had been waiting for someone like him, but at what price?

"Please give this a chance. We will be okay."

I agreed and from that point on we started taking precautions. Things like checking the cars before we got inside, watching for someone following us, and checking in regularly. After a couple of weeks and months, things seemed to be falling into place. We were happy; still learning from each other, but less scared at this point.

A few months later, I get a letter saying my ex-husband was incarcerated. I had no idea why. The letter was standard protocol for someone with a restraining order. I was happy to know he was not coming near us any time soon, and we didn't have to watch our backs any more for the time being.

I found my prince charming, the man who changed my life, the man I wanted to spend the rest of my life with. He loves me unconditionally no matter my flaws. Plus, he encourages me to follow my dreams. I decided to take him home to meet my family, and they loved him. We took a vacation and visited extended family in Mexico. They were unaware of my past with my ex-husband and they assumed Octavio was Angel's biological dad. Everyone would comment on how well Octavio cared for his "son". The relief was unbelievable, I was not blinded by love and he was the person I thought he was with my son. Not only did I see it but others saw it and that made me happy.

When you are single and find someone, who loves your baby or babies the way you wished for, then you should consider it like winning the lottery. We became the family I always had growing up. On Angel's second birthday, he helped pay for the party, along with his school expenses. He would buy him clothes, shoes and took him for haircuts. At the time, he still lived with his mom, Uvita; she is one of two mothers-in-law that I have. He also has his mom Laura, who adopted him as an adult, under special circumstances.

The blessing of two moms pours on all of us as a family. We have double the love with them. Our kids have three grandmas instead of two, we celebrate the holidays twice, have twice the food, and twice the gifts, to name just a few.

Fast-forward to three years later: I was still working two jobs, part-time cosmetology, and real estate.

Octavio was still living with his mom Uvita and I
was living with my parents. My real estate career
was not where I wanted it to be yet, so I had to work
two jobs. By this time, I had left my ex-mother in
law's salon and was only working three days at a
different barbershop. I now had more flexible hours
to spend with Angel. Octavio was working at a law
firm and on his associate's degree at the same time.
We saw each other as much as we could due to our
busy schedules. At times it was only for an hour or
so because we both worked and he went to school in
the evening, but he always made time to see us.
Even when it was cold and dark in the winter he
would stop by before going home.

In December of 2009, Octavio and I found out we
were pregnant. We would be having another bundle
of joy. It was time for us to move in together and
prepare for the arrival of our baby. We saved money
and decided to buy a home. My prince charming
would become my client, and after only looking at a
few houses, we decided we had found the one. We
moved in March and our beautiful, perfect baby girl

was born in August 2010. After twelve hours of labor, we finally met our baby, and we named her Emily Marie. Emily is everything Octavio and I are together. She is kind and smart like him, independent and dedicated like me, and as happy as Octavio and I are together. She is the icing on the cake and keeps us on our toes.

Octavio not only changed my life but Angel's life as well. Before Emily was born, he decided he wanted to adopt Angel legally and give him his last name. He said he didn't want to have two babies with different last names and since Angel's biological dad was not in the picture, he thought it was time to make this move. We hired an attorney with the help of my other mother-in-law Laura and started the process of adoption. It was easier than we thought since Joe, who by this time was out of prison, declined his rights to Angel. He never even attended court. Angel became Octavio's son before Emily was born. We went out and celebrated at our favorite place, Olive Garden.

Octavio holds both his kids by the hand and guides them together, pushes them to be the best they can be, challenges them academically, and rewards them the same. I cannot imagine my life without my husband. We talk about our dreams and goals and plan for the future with our kids' best interests in mind. He changed me; he gave us an opportunity for a better life. The results of my dreams. I took a leap of faith and found a good man. The man I hope to spend the rest of my life with and the man I thank for loving us the way he does.

Looking back at everything I have learned when dating and the conversations that I have had with many other people, it has taken me to the conclusion that relationships should also be looked at as a business. Like I said before when I was dating, I didn't know what questions to ask for or what to look for. One assumes everything will eventually fall into place once you find someone you fall in love with, but how can you fall in love with someone you don't really know or look forward to knowing? In the past fifteen years, I have had many friends and clients in both cosmetology and real estate who have separated or divorced from their significant others because things didn't work out as they expected.

This is the reason I say that when you date, it should be looked at as a business. Your life is your "business." Ask yourself what are you looking for in a partner. Don't be afraid to ask questions. Once you date someone and are attracted to that person and are ready for other dates, follow up with more serious questions. Just like if you were interviewing a candidate for vice-president of your "company." The sooner you ask those questions the sooner you will get to the bottom of things and on to the next.

Always ask what they will bring to the table and make sure that that will make you happy. Be honest with them and yourself ALWAYS! Ask questions such as: What do you expect from a partner? What are your goals or ambitions? How close are you to your family? Why haven't your past relationships worked out and what have you learned from them?

How often do you like to go out and where do you like to go when going out? What makes you happy? What makes you mad or sad? How important are your friend's vs your partner? What are your priorities and where do you see yourself in five years? What do you think about children, do you have any, or do you plan on having any? If there are kids involved talk about it at the beginning. Do you have custody of the kid/s? How will it affect us financially? Do you drink or do any type of drugs I should be aware of? Discuss what is expected from one another and what is not, but do it fairly.

Once you are in a serious relationship, continue to treat it as a business, with a win-win mentality. My broker Michael Coburn from RE/MAX Town & Country in Allen, TX has taught us to use this mentality with our clients. This idea can also be applied at home with your life and "business" partner. This basically means that in real estate, I want my client to win in every aspect of the real estate transaction. By accomplishing this, my client wins and is happy, therefore I win as well. Your relationship and/or marriage is a business of two. Everything one does affect the other. Both should treat it with that win-win mentality. Treat each other with the same love and respect you expect to receive.

In business, everything is negotiable! The same goes for a relationship. Learn to negotiate with your partner. Once you have moved on to the next level and are serious about the relationship and moved in together, there is still work to do. There is no such thing as a perfect relationship, but with a little bit of work, it can be a great one.

Learn to negotiate with your partner. For example, my husband and I agreed he would pay the mortgage and I would pay the bills. This way we wouldn't argue about who is paying what at home or what we are spending our money on. I wash the dishes and he takes out the trash. I help our kids with math homework and he helps with the reading. I wash clothes and he folds them. Even sex can be negotiated. For example, there have been days that I am extremely tired and he offers to let me sleep in late the next morning and not make him breakfast if we spend some time together that night. There are days where not everything works out normally, we are not robots and we haven't programmed ourselves to do everything we negotiate. Sometimes I have to take out the trash, he has to cook or let me sleep, but we understand things happen and we have to help each other out where one left off.

For some couples, negotiating can be one person works and pays all the bills while the other one stays home to maintain order, clean, cook, and/or care for the children. Other negotiations can be how you spend the holidays with each other's family. For example, my husband and I pick whose family we will be with at midnight for Christmas and then we switch to the other family for New Year's. Unless we celebrate it at our house, then we invite both families. So, with that being said, how you spend your time with your family and friends either individually or together can also be negotiated. The key here is to do everything fairly with one another.

Whatever works for you as long as you are both in agreement and are happy with the results. If one way doesn't work, try a different approach. As long as you both love and agree with one another, everything is negotiable.

It is reported that the most commonly reported cause of divorce in America is a lack of commitment. Don't be a statistic; communicate with the person you chose to be in love with, and negotiate.

Self-Reflection

After marrying Octavio, I realized that even though we love each other so much there is still work we have to do within our marriage to keep it going. We both have to be willing to do the work and this is where negotiating comes in handy. Do the work with a partner who wants to do the work just as much as you do. That's why it is a very important part of the process to "interview" the people you date, thus narrowing your options to someone more compatible with you.

I have a close friend who calls me super woman because of everything I manage to do daily, but I can't be super woman if I don't have a superman beside me. My husband is my superman. Make sure you find your superman who makes you feel like super woman or vice versa.

I have met someone and the first date has been arranged. What questions can I ask on this date to know if this relationship should continue?

How can I manage my emotions to stay on track
with keeping this relationship balanced?

_____

_____

_____

If I am uncomfortable in any way, can I walk away?

_____

_____

_____

Can I work well with this person as a team?

_____

_____

_____

Chapter Four:

The Gift of Friendships

"You cannot choose your family, but you can pick your friends, so choose wisely because they are a gift from God."- Jorge Sanchez

One thing I learned in life from my dad: he was right when he told us to choose our friends wisely. He would say that sometimes people don't get along with family members because we all have different personalities, goals, and ambitions. But God gave us friends as a gift and you can pick and choose who you want in your life.

I have applied my dad's thought to my idea that everything in life should be treated as a business. By this, I do not mean you should only have friends whom you will benefit from. I mean people should have friends that will be a positive influence and will learn and grow together as a team. Friendships are relationships that, if treated as a business, can be very beneficial to both parties. In many cases, friends sometimes become closer than your own family. But you have to make sure that both are giving the same energy to one another. Make sure it is not a one-way toxic relationship where one is always the listener, the helper, the adviser, babysitter, or the giver. As they say, friendships are a two-way street, if not, then it's a free ride.

The majority of the time there are five people you can consider your friends, people you can count on, and people you can party with. My husband and I have those five friends who now have families of their own and some of their children are older than ours. We have all become like families because we enjoy their company, we have mutual respect for them, and most importantly, they are people that we can trust around Angel and Emily. They are people that we know are a positive influence in our children's lives. At times, they have even given us good advice and we will do the same for their children. As you get older, you learn what is important in a friendship and how much you can give but also receive. You become more selective of the people you wish to go to a club or a bar with and also the people you can invite home to a cookout or a barbeque.

If I would have treated my friendships like a business when I was younger, I would have avoided many sleepless nights worrying about friends who were out drinking and driving, or helping others with their homework because they chose to go out instead of doing the homework. All of this is part of growing up and trying to fit in and have friends. One important issue I want to stress is, some relationships will continue to grow into adulthood, while others become toxic and it's imperative to let go of these people and move on. If we treated them as a business, many of us would have "fired" some of these friends a long time ago.

Make sure you choose them wisely because a good friendship is like a fairytale; they are there once upon a time and will be there until forever after. Such is the case with my best friend.

I have been lucky to have a best friend who has been there for me since I was fifteen years old. He has become my brother and Angel and Emily call him uncle Mijio, but his full name is Remijio Urena.

We met in high school: he was a sophomore and I was a freshman. The funny thing is, at the time, he had a best friend whom I had a crush on, and I had a friend he had a crush on. The connection brought us together as good friends. As you can see, we both benefited from the relationship. He married my friend Anita and together have two amazing children, Bella and Prince. They recently celebrated their 20th anniversary together.

Mijio is the type of friend who will never leave you behind. It doesn't matter who you are. He will check on you if you are having any problems, he will ask how your day is even if you're a stranger at a store. He will always make sure he provides support to his family, friends, and coworkers in any way they need, whether it's for work or home.

As a matter of fact, Mijio was there for me during my involvement with Joe. I recall one time when we had a huge fight.

Joe had hit me, leaving me face down on the bedroom floor, after which, he pulled his gun out and pointed it at the back of my head. "I am going to shoot you in the head."

Then he suddenly pointed the gun at the floor and pulled the trigger. I felt the shot go through the floor next to my ear; it left my ears ringing for a few minutes. I was speechless just waiting for him to shoot me. Instead, he got up and started knocking everything off our dresser with his gun and yelling how I had pushed his buttons. It was my fault, again. All I remember was him getting upset over some food I served him for dinner and I wasn't ready to eat with him. He knocked the plate with food off the table and screamed for me to clean up the mess. My crying got him more upset and that led to him hitting me and my landing on the floor.

As he was breaking things, throwing them around the bedroom, I noticed he was bleeding. I got up, sat on the bed, and asked him to calm down because he had hurt himself. Instead of calming down, he grabbed my backpack which was full of my cosmetology books and threw it at me. He demanded I be quiet. At this time, a small fire broke out in the living room from a gas heater that was attached to the wall with vents. We immediately focused our attention on putting out the fire. Apparently, a car had crashed against a gas line in the neighborhood and it caused a lot of small fires around the area. We started to hear sirens, ambulances, and fire trucks, coming to the crash site and other homes where the fires were bigger than ours.

I noticed Joe got nervous, and once our fire was out, he said "I don't want to be around you right now." He left.

At the time, I had no idea where he might be headed and didn't care much. I got my cell phone and called my best friend Mijio.

We discussed the incident at length. He informed me, "Maria this was too close a call. You have to get out of there. One of these times, he's going to kill you."

He was very disturbed but knew that if he was there when Joe got home there would be problems. Joe is about five feet six-seven inches, and Mijio was a mad five-foot-eleven man who could easily hurt him if needed, but neither one of us wanted things to get to that point.

"I'm going to have Anita pick you up. Get a bag packed and put it outside, don't waste any time. He could be home any minute."

I needed to make sure Joe was not anywhere in sight before she came over. I knew how Joe's truck sounded and could hear him from a distance. So, I knew if it was safe for her to park out front and pick me up. We decided I would be safer at Anita's parents' home because Joe didn't know where they lived. She spoke with her mom and she agreed to let me stay there for the night. This is an act of kindness that I will never forget and will cherish for the rest of my life.

The next day, Mijio picked me up; I wanted to get far away from Joe, so I decided to go to Milwaukee. I was ashamed of my situation, and the last thing I wanted was to tell my parents what happened. Deep down, I thought it was love and didn't want my family to hate him. Mijio took me to the bus stop, gave me money, and I left for Wisconsin. My parents' immediate family were in Milwaukee. I decided to tell my parents I was on vacation for a few days, or weeks if necessary until I returned.

My best friend is a brother from another mother, and he carried me during the darkest time in my life. He helped me like a brother helps his sister, gave me advice without criticism, guided me, and gave me the tools needed to build my confidence. Mijio helped me understand it was not my fault, then encouraged me to do better. Since high school, he had been there for me, no matter what the circumstance. The best part about our relationship is, he tells me the truth, even if it's not what I want to hear and I do the same for him. To this day, twenty-three years later from when our friendship started, we remain encouraged by each other; neither one ever feels unsupported. This is what makes it a good friendship.

When friends are dedicated to each other, they give advice, make suggestions, or just be there in a time of crisis without expectations. We set goals together and make friendly competitions such as who burns more calories in one day, who can walk the longest, and even who can finish paying off their home mortgage first with their spouses. All four of us including Anita and my husband have paid off our homes and always cheer one another's success and accomplishments. We have a mutual love and respect for our families and know we can count on each other for whatever is needed. We love and care for each other's children as if they were our own.

On the other side of the coin, staying away from a toxic friend or family member can be difficult. If saying no to someone is a challenge then saying goodbye can be even more difficult, but it's necessary to find true peace and success. This is why I have learned friendships should also be treated as a business. Just take, for instance, breaking up with a friend when it's not healthy or fulfilling. Then, you need to understand that treating a relationship like a business will help give you that push on whether or not it's beneficial. Weigh the pros and cons and make the decision that will benefit your life the most, as if it was your business and you were either making or losing money. It doesn't necessarily mean making money because you don't benefit monetarily from a friend, but it means how healthy the relationship is for you. Do they invest time in you as much as you invest in them, do they treat you fairly like you treat them, do they help you and positively advise you as you do for them? Are you both goal-oriented and push each other towards those mutual goals?

One such example deals with my mom. I, unfortunately, had to unfriend her on social media, along with two or three family members. My mom was posting things that not only did I disagree with but hurt me as her daughter. So, for my peace of mind, I made the decision. To unfriend a loved one or stop socializing with them doesn't mean you stop loving them, it simply means you don't want to continue getting hurt one way or another. Sometimes people say things that they don't mean, at the time, especially on social media. They want to take it back and apologize after you have been hurt, but the way they made you feel cannot be changed, and for that reason, it's just better to simply stay away.

It is a difficult time in America with a lot of hatred and racism. We hear it all day every day, including television, radio, and social media. Lately, I have also decided to unfriend some of my "friends"/work associates on social media with whom I don't share political views on certain subjects. They express hatred in their posts. We have to respect other people's opinions and views, but sometimes it becomes too blunt to continue seeing daily. Fortunately, we have a button to unfollow and delete people. I will not argue with them because we all have the freedom to use our First Amendment, which is freedom of speech. I will respect their opinion just like I want my opinion to be respected, but I also have the freedom to not hear or see what they are posting by simply unfollowing them or unfriending them. There is no need to fight or argue with anyone because that is their opinion. It needs to be respected as much as your opinion, but that doesn't mean you must accept the message.

The problem with social media bullying among our children is growing. Let's teach them that it is okay to unfriend and unfollow those people who are doing the bullying or the threads or negative comments about them. We must teach them to choose their friends wisely, and everyone has an opinion. Our job is to respect their choices, but they do not have a right to directly harm anyone physically or mentally with their views. Let's teach them they have the freedom to be selective because their friends are a gift to us from God, and we are the same as them. Therefore, choosing good friends is very important.

We talk to Angel and Emily about friends and we advise them that they can gain and lose many things with the friends they choose, and whether they win or lose is up to them. Parents must lead by example, and learn to see friendships like a business. Then we must teach that to our children if we want them to have successful relationships in life. It's better to have one good friend than ten who can't care less about your wellbeing. Let's learn to choose quality over quantity in friendships, and the only way to do so is by treating them like a business with a win-win mentality.

Self-Reflection

Friends help us in many stages of our lives and we must do the same for them: Be there when they need you, help them when you know they need it, listen when they have a problem, and carry them when they have fallen. But make sure you find that support in them when it's your turn to be carried because, for me, that is what helped me out of a dark hole where I was.

Does my current friend list benefit both parties? Or, are my friendships one-sided?

_____

_____

_____

Do my friends contact me for more than help?

_____

_____

_____

Do they make excuses every time I ask for help?

_____

_____

_____

Do they challenge me to be a better person?

_____

_____

_____

Do they help me achieve my goals through support?

_____

_____

_____

Chapter Five:

Reap What You Sow

"Speak to your children as if they are the wisest,
kindest, most beautiful and magical humans on
earth, for what they believe is what they will
become."-Brooke Hampton

A short time ago, I had a conversation with my son, Angel. The question did not surprise me, knowing my son. He asked, "Mom what happens if I don't believe in God? Would you be mad at me?"

We have always been a very close family, so now and then my children have questions that I'm sure they ponder in their little heads before they ask.

Octavio and I had been taking them to communion classes for the last two years. After completing their first communion, Angel started taking his confirmation class, so questions about God are very common during this time. To be honest, neither of them is too happy to go to class on a Sunday morning and have extra homework during the week, so his question didn't bother nor surprise me. My husband and I are very open with our children, we discuss everything you can think of and are happy to listen when they ask questions. Some of them are not ones we would have talked about with our parents.

In our household, we start every morning with "good morning my beautiful daughter" and "good morning my handsome son." They give me a kiss, and my husband when he is home or comes home from work. When they are asleep, Octavio peeks through their doors to see them before he leaves for work. The love and respect he shows his kids are unconditional and like no other.

I will never forget him chasing them around the house with them screaming to get away, or pretending to be asleep to surprise him. The routine was an everyday occurrence after school. To this day, they continue some similar interactions.

However, with Angel being as tall as his dad is now, they have moved on to play wrestling. Before bed, Octavio kisses them both goodnight and gives them his blessing. Emily is ten now and thinks she's too grown to play with Daddy but likes to sit or lay next to him while we watch TV. At times, she will bring him her famous peanut butter jelly sandwich in bed to show him how much she cares for him. It has become a new bonding time. I love seeing them together and hope that one day their love, trust, and respect is as mutual as my relationship with my dad.

My husband is the reason our life runs so smoothly; he is kind, calm, patient, loving, and transmits that to us all. We both agree that our kids are our main priority and spending as much time with them will help us achieve our goals. Our happiness comes from teaching them right from wrong; it must be the main focus. One parental responsibility I take very seriously is making time for our children. My real estate career is done during the day while they are in school, then I pick them up and go home to spend time with them while I cook and/or clean.

Occasionally, I have had to meet clients after school hours, so they come along for the ride. If I have to meet a client in the evening, I wait until Octavio is home and I leave again. When I am not seeing clients, we watch TV, cook, or bake desserts together. In the summers, we often go out for a walk, play tennis or walk our recent new member of the family, Max, our Shih Tzu. The main reason I chose to get a real estate license is flexibility. I can work my schedule and thus far it has worked perfectly for us.

If you 'treat life like a business,' investing in your children does not require planning or thinking ahead, it becomes second nature. 'Reap what you sow.' When your main focus is your children, seeing them succeed results from your guidance. It's a win-win mentality; if your children are successful, then you both win in life.

Imagine your child is a very popular name brand, let's take for example, Nike. I'm sure that the founder's Bill Bowerman and Phil Knight didn't know how big their brand (baby) would be, but they envisioned, just like any business owner (or parent) does, that their creation (child) or idea would be very successful one day. They worked hard to guide their business in the best way possible and faced many obstacles on the way to finally achieve what they envisioned and more. The same idea can be applied to our children. My father always told me that his goal in life was for his four children to achieve greater things than him. This is very much like the song I previously described.

My dad came to the United States in 1985 and received legal residency through the amnesty given by Ronald Reagan in 1986. He speaks some English, but most importantly, he is the hardest working, most honest person I know. My dad says that a parent's goal should be to make sure that our children are better than us in every way. One of his goals by immigrating to the United States from Michoacán, Mexico, was to have a better life. He believes the only way for an immigrant to achieve success is by working twice as hard as anyone else.

In fact, his heritage, education, and language barriers made his task even more difficult.

I remember their first home and how excited he was. He told me, "Look, we bought a house, not too big, but it's a decent size for us. It doesn't have a car garage, but the house is new and I'm happy. I want you to one day have a bigger house than this one because you are better than me. You speak English and you go to school here, therefore you should achieve greater things in life than I have."

I will never forget his words and I give my children the same message. Our children should be a better version of us. As the years pass with my father's encouragement, we can give our children some of the things we never had. The concept further enhances my message, to have a win-win mentality.

The concept has further paid off with Angel being clear on the idea of going to Harvard to become a surgeon. He took high school credits this year in middle school and is hoping to graduate high school early with an associate's degree, due to a program called Early College High School. We started pushing Angel when he was in second or third grade. He was usually a straight-A student and occasionally would get a B.

We always paid attention to his grades and urged him to do better. The school he attended sent a newsletter stating students had access to the onsite learning platform; they could practice, if necessary, on a particular subject, thereby improving their skills on specific subjects.

We made a deal with Angel since he brought home a B. He would log onto the website and spend thirty minutes a day on the subject in which he got the B. By doing so, we knew that the practice would help him improve for the next six weeks. Needless to say, he was not thrilled with this idea. Because he dislikes homework, he agreed not to get any more Bs. Our lesson was how to negotiate a deal with him, just like in business. We do it in a way that sounds interesting to him and makes him feel like he has a say so in it. We started with one hour and he brought it down to thirty minutes. To us, thirty minutes is sufficient but we wanted to start high so he felt like he had an input in the negotiation. If you feel thirty minutes is not enough then start with ninety minutes for example and negotiate down to a time you feel will suffice.

The next phase was Angel wanting an iPhone 11 when he was in eighth grade. Octavio and I had planned to give it to him for Christmas as a reward for him excelling in school. During this time Angel brought home a B; he used the excuse of being too busy in school. He was in 8th grade taking gifted and talented classes, high school credits, president of his school's student council, and member of the advanced orchestra. Octavio used this as leverage and they both came to an agreement and signed a contract. It stated that his dad would buy the phone the day it was released but for each B Angel brought home every six weeks he would pay his dad $100 towards the phone. This encouraged Angel since Christmas was two months away and he didn't want to wait until then to get it.

Any parent can use this as an example to negotiate alternatives with their children. Plan: if you know you are planning on buying them something for no reason or if they are asking for something, use this time to negotiate with them. Maybe negotiate school grades or chores at home you need them to fulfill. This way you both feel you accomplished something at the same time and they get the feeling of earning what they wanted.

Angel's desire to save money urged him to turn his Bs into As. He started asking the teachers for extra credit to raise his grades so he wouldn't pay $100. Every time Angel got his progress reports, he would work; that process helped us teach him accountability and responsibility. By the end of the year, he only paid his dad $400, which was from his birthday, Christmas, and allowance money.

When Angel and Emily were little, we would reward them for their report cards by taking them to Walmart so they could pick one toy each. The deal stated if they got all as it was a $100.00 limit. Lucky for us, they never chose a toy that expensive.

But if they brought home a B, it dropped to a $50 limit. Emily has never brought us a B so she has been fortunate to always get what she wants as a reward. Emily also has a busy school schedule at a young age. Once a week she travels to another school, with a group that excels and needs higher learning education. She is also bilingual, so at the end of the day, she goes with a bilingual teacher for about forty minutes. This year she will be a fifth-grader and won't be in bilingual classes, but we told her she will substitute it with another program offered at the school such as a reading club, choir, violin-like Angel - or anything else that interests her.

As they got older, they didn't want any more toys so we let them choose, for example, an amusement park or their restaurant of choice. We always look for ways to encourage and reward them, which we believe has been working for our family. The important thing is picking rewards that fit your budget. I know growing up neither my nor Octavio's parents had the money to buy us a $100 toy, but we were satisfied with a $10 toy. The point is to reward your kids when they do a good job.

As a parent, you are the CEO, you run their life (your business). They are smart, but you are smarter, and you know what they like and dislike. You negotiate and set the rules. It can take time but someone will eventually give in, just make sure it's the child. They like to be praised for their good actions and rewarded in some fashion. If you are going out to lunch or dinner for the weekend, tell them it's because they did something good during the week. When you communicate, make sure the conversations are positive, even if you have had a bad day. Do not make them a sounding board. Children thrive when they hear how smart and handsome or beautiful, they are. Believe in them, so they can believe in themselves. But most importantly, tell them "I love you" every day.

Your next routine is telling them how you see the future; maybe a doctor, pilot, singer, or whatever their dream is. Tell them how you see them flying the biggest airplane, doing the most important surgery, or on stage singing to thousands of people. It is important to help them see their vision and how to work on it. I hug Angel and I tell him that I already see him being the best surgeon he can be and performing some of the most important surgeries in the world. Angel and Emily want to go to Harvard. So, we bought Angel a Harvard hat that he wears and Emily a small teddy bear wearing a Harvard shirt. Always remember to dream big. One way to succeed is by envisioning the future you desire, then doing the work to make it happen.

It is exciting to know the most important people in our lives share the same idea of our children's success and that they are our biggest investment. By this, I do not mean we will invest money in them, it all comes down to the time, dedication, teachings, and quality over quantity we give them. For example, my best friend Mijio, and I set a goal in 2018. Our income ratio was alright but not at the level we wanted, so we challenged each other to increase our yearly income to 100k. Mijio picked up a second job at the time and was sure he would beat me to our goal. He worked hard weekdays and weekends and was able to accomplish another goal we had, which was to pay off our houses that year.

Mijio was usually home by the time his son and daughter got home from school. Prince, his son, usually wanted to play video games or play ball with his dad. But, during those months, his son went to bed sad, missing his father. At times, Prince wouldn't go to sleep until his dad got home at night and Mijio wasn't too happy knowing his son was up possibly waiting for him late on school nights until around ten or eleven at night.

In the end, the effort paid off, and Mijio beat me to make 100k first. The income continued to increase, well into the next year, until he saw how much time he'd missed being with his family and chose to back off due to the damage it was doing at home. He let go of his second job and focused on his family over the money. It was clear to him that making a lot of money was not as important as spending time with his family. As for me, I am fortunate enough to have also accomplished my goal the following year and became a top agent with my broker. I earned a certificate for becoming one of the top 5 agents at the beginning of 2020, but to me, being a top agent now is not as important as being the best mom I can be. One day, our children will be leaving home, and that is when I can focus on being a top agent once again. At this point, taking care of our household, cooking warm meals, going to after school activities, and keeping a clean environment at home is a higher priority.

Another outstanding example is my twenty-four-year-old sister Miriam. She recently separated from her fiancé and has three babies, my munchkins: five-year-old Jordan and four-year-old twins Anthony and Jonathan. She was attending Texas A&M, working on her bachelor's degree before her separation. Afterward, she started working, struggling to find the perfect job to provide for her kids. After a couple of attempts, it seemed she found the perfect opportunity. Mimi (short for Miriam) worked as a parole officer for a juvenile center, and she was happy and making decent money. She had a schedule where she could take the kids to school in the mornings and our dad would pick them up after school. The job had its drawbacks, working in a juvenile center with children who have committed murder and other crimes are free to roam around like any other school. Parole officers don't have a weapon or taser, nor can they use force to restrain them because they are considered minors. But with her love and patience for these kids, she was able to gain their trust and friendship. After a while, she didn't feel as threatened as she did at the beginning. My little sister is the strongest person I know mentally and physically, but this job was something to worry about. She doesn't let fear get in her way and her courage and determination have taken her a long way. The job, unfortunately, required her to change shifts, and she was not willing to make that sacrifice, as it would force her to spend less time with her children. My dad has always told us that our kids are more important than anything else, and she agreed. Mimi's persistence allowed her to find another job that offered an opportunity to take the kids to school and be with them before school, along with dropping them off. Her salary dropped, but the quality of time she can spend with her kids makes the sacrifice worthwhile. My sister is a compassionate, courteous, and loving person, hence the reason she can make the sacrifice. Plus, because of the support system in place with our family, she is never alone. Mimi challenges herself to be as independent as she can be, and I admire her dearly for it.

Sometimes you need to balance the scale between the needs and wants. It is very difficult to accomplish the wants when you are a single parent, but focusing on what is most important and managing your time and money wisely can help you spend the time with your kids as you desire. I, for example, worked a full-time job and did on-line classes once Angel fell asleep so that I would be able to have more freedom and spend time with him in the future. I did so for a year with very little sleep, but in the end, it was all worth it. It's a little harder for my sister because she has three kids to care for; she has put her bachelor's on hold and is planning on taking a training class so she can maybe start her own business in the beauty industry. Additionally, Covid-19 and on-line school learning for the kids have pushed her to make some changes. Once again, she had to quit her job, otherwise, the kids couldn't attend online classes, and she was told by the school that her kids would fail the year if she didn't do online classes with them. Fortunately, she has saved some money and will start esthetician classes soon and take advantage of her time at home.

Like my sister, you should plan on how you can better yourself, what classes or courses can you take to help you get a better job, career, or maybe start your own business. Envision how you see yourself in 3-5 years, be patient and persistent and God willing, you will be there in a blink of an eye. Ask for financial aid that can help you through the classes or the course. Ask for any assistance possible to make your load less heavy.

If you are still wondering about my answer to Angel's question on God, keep reading. I explained: "You know I love God above anything else. He has given me everything I have in life; He gave me you and Emily and for that, I love Him with all my heart. I love God more than I love anything or anyone because, without Him, neither you nor Emily would be with us. I love Him for all the opportunities He gives us every day. We do not have a mansion, but we have a home. We don't have the latest model car, but we have a car. We have work to provide for our needs, some wants, and we are healthy enough to continue working to keep providing. We are thankful to God for everything that we have and don't yet have." The conversation paused. "I know you are not at this level of relationship with God yet, but neither was I at your age. All I can do for you is provide you the information you need to help you decide what you want later in life. For now, we will continue to take you to confirmation classes so you can learn about Him and the Bible, and I will tell you about my experiences with God. There will come a time when you will decide based on this information if you believe in Him or not."

It is important to give your children the freedom to explore their feelings. But, on the other hand, you as a parent must continue to provide them the proper channels to develop the tools necessary to succeed.

It is impossible to foresee the future, however with God's help, we hope for the best. Then, either way, we did our best as parents and it was not because we failed in raising them. Like all humans, they have to make their own decisions, right or wrong. It's their choice.

Self-Reflection

How can I provide a better life for my child?

_____

_____

_____

How can I improve my relationship with God to make better decisions?

_____

_____

_____

Am I a cheerleader in my kid's life?

_____

_____

_____

Do I take the necessary time out of my day to spend quality time with my kids?

_____

_____

_____

Chapter Six:

Thirty Minutes Worth the Investment

"He who has health has hope, and he who has hope has everything."-Arabian Proverb

One summer afternoon in 2018, a phone call made me realize how close our family came to losing my dad. He called and stated they were taking him to the hospital; stage three kidney failure. The call scared me in many ways. I knew my dad was a Type II diabetic for the past twenty years, but this was different. My dad worked very hard every day, never missed a beat, and the idea of him being this sick I found unbelievable. Earlier that year, my mom took him to the hospital for chest pain. It turned out that his heart was fine, but one of his kidneys had stopped working and the other one was headed in the same direction.

My dad couldn't believe the doctors. He is the type of person to only see a doctor when he can't handle the pain any longer, which usually isn't common. On this specific day, he said that during dialysis he lost consciousness and the nurses called an ambulance. My mom and sister drove as fast as they could to get to the dialysis center. My sister arrived before I did, and he didn't recognize her or hear what

she said to him. I arrived a few minutes later and was sad to see my dad in that condition. A few minutes later he was transported to Parkland Hospital in Dallas, where we met with him and the doctors.

My dad had a tough year, and I am sure the rest of the family felt that way too. An illness this severe in any family can be devastating, seeing someone you love hurting breaks you inside. Once they started doing tests to confirm what the doctors suspected, my dad said several times he had no symptoms to indicate that his kidney was failing. I took him to see three different nephrologists to convince him they were not lying. They all did blood work and gave him the same results: stage three kidney failure.

The last doctor that we saw at Baylor Medical Center in Dallas was kind, soft-spoken, and compassionate and said the right words that made him realize he was ill and needed help. Dr. Catalina Sanchez-Hanson spoke his language and had a heartfelt conversation with him. She explained how his kidneys failed because of diabetes: one had completely shrunk and was no longer working and the other was working at a bare minimum.

We figured since my dad was always so busy working, his body was used to his busy lifestyle and he didn't pay attention to any symptoms. He had swollen feet for the past two years but he was ok with it, assuming it was a side effect of his diabetes. Dr. Catalina also referred my dad to Dr. Ahmer Younas. He is an oncologist in Rowlett, TX. My dad had to get tested for possible cancer in his kidneys. Dr. Younas is kindhearted and very amiable. He greets you with a smile and takes his time explaining the tests and what to expect. The empathy he shows is amazing, but at the same time, he comforts you. He shared our pain and fears, yet he assured us that my dad would be okay.

My son Angel went with us to the second appointment and Angel mentioned he wanted to be a surgeon. A year later, Dr. Younas asked about Angel, and if he was continuing with his plans of being a surgeon. I was so impressed by his memory and the fact he truly cared.

As soon as my dad was notified of his kidneys and took time off work for tests and different doctor opinions, the side effects of his kidney failure caught up to him. His whole body started swelling and began retaining fluids drastically within two weeks. He was afraid of eating or drinking because he would end up in the hospital once a week to drain his fluids. Then, his stomach became swollen and hard, and he could barely drink one glass of water a day.

When we first met Dr. Hansen, my dad's kidney function was around 24% and she immediately suggested dialysis, but my dad refused. The last thing my dad wanted was to feel useless. No matter what was happening, he refused to accept the illness. One month went by and his kidney function dropped to 14%. By this time, he was no longer working and Dr. Hansen convinced him to start dialysis.

My dad is a warrior. He wanted to do dialysis at home so he could work, but my mom felt it would be very complicated. So, my dad drove to the dialysis center instead. They set him up for every other day. We could see him feeling defeated little by little, the sound in his voice was obvious. I called after every dialysis day. He would try to keep himself busy at home doing yard work, cleaning, and cooking, but it was not enough. My dad is the type of person who only takes one straight week off work because he gets bored at home, so being confined every day was very difficult for him.

During this time, my parents divorced. After almost 30 years of marriage, they decided it was best for them to part. They were no longer a team and didn't love each other the way a couple should. My mom moved out because she wanted my father to keep the house. They had a very friendly divorce; my mom got her half of what the house was worth and half of my dad's 401K. Neither one of them fought more than the other and were content with their decision.

They see each other at family gatherings and are respectful. Of course, they are not best friends anymore but are cordial, the way I feel every divorced couple should behave. I admire my parents' decision to get a divorce. They had lost interest in each other and were no longer in love. If there is hope to find happiness with someone else, please do so. As long as there is life, there is hope to be happy with someone else of your choosing. I reminded them that we are all grown, my siblings and I and that we can take care of ourselves and they needed to take care of themselves. My parents are in their early fifties and God willing, they have many years of life and happiness ahead of them. I mean, who wants to see their parents old and alone with no one to share a day with, a meal, a party? We can only do so much as their children, but I'm sure they would love to have another companion for the rest of their lives.

My dad lost track of himself to give us a better life. I can remember how hard he worked to provide a better life for his family. He never complained and was happy to give us what he could afford. Plus, we lived within our means. My dad is a simple man, well-mannered, soft-spoken, and a man of a few words unless he is talking to us. He gives great advice and wants us to count on him as a father and a friend. It is because of my dad that I strive every day to be the best person I can be as an example for my children to follow. He is my hero.

I mentioned the fear of losing my father in the beginning; my dad knew he was a diabetic, and yet he ignored his health and diet while being a good provider. He had been placed on insulin since he was diagnosed with Type II diabetes. My dad thought working hard daily counted as having an active life. There was never time for him to walk, run, or workout. But I remember my dad being active when we were little. He is the reason I like sports and used to take us to the park to ride bikes, to play soccer and basketball. I remember him being on a soccer team with his friends. My mom would take us to see him play. My dad and I used to watch soccer games together on some weekends, especially Mexico vs the USA. Later on, my brothers Juan and Jorge (Guero) were more into football than soccer so my dad and I bonded during this time. My brothers played football in middle school and put soccer aside.

I remember FIFA World Cup 2002 took place in Japan and my dad and I used to wake up at three in the morning to watch the Mexico games, and then he would go to work afterward. Unfortunately, my dad stopped playing and being active. Maybe this is the reason he ended up with kidney failure. He didn't exercise anymore, didn't follow a diet nor try to eat healthily.

After seeing my dad's lifestyle and health deteriorate like many of us have, I can also conclude that life should be treated like a business. Health is an investment and should be looked at in that way. You need not pay for a gym membership to stay healthy, although now you can be a member at a gym for as low as ten dollars a month. Just walking 30 minutes a day is a great investment in your health. In that time, walking or working out can help reduce the risk of cardiovascular diseases, high cholesterol, and even Type II diabetes. There is a study that shows that Type II diabetes can cost over $125,000 to be treated over a lifetime. If we simply walk thirty minutes a day, we can reduce the chance of cardiovascular diseases, high cholesterol, and Type II diabetes. We can reduce stress, strengthen bones and muscles and it helps improve balance and coordination. I call that a great investment; thirty minutes a day can help with all that was previously mentioned.

The American Diabetes Association released an article saying people with diabetes spend approximately $16,750 per year on medical expenses and more than half that amount is strictly related to diabetes. As a business person, I would rather spend $10 per month in a gym to avoid having to spend that much more money on treatment yearly in the future. One vial of insulin costs approximately $300/month without insurance. In 1999, one vial of insulin was $21 but increased to $332 per vial in 2019. Once again, I would rather walk for thirty minutes or join a gym for way less than 1 vial of insulin a month. This is just considering the costs for Type II diabetes and not any other condition combined.

It is believed that working out at least thirty minutes a day improves memory and brain function, aids in weight management can help combat cancer-related fatigue, and reduces feelings of anxiety and depression.

My dad also lost some of his sight during this time and was diagnosed with diabetic retinopathy. He had to have cataracts removed and experienced internal retinal bleeding due to his high glucose levels. The doctor called for several laser surgeries to close some vessels in his eyes that were causing the bleeding and eventually he had surgery in one of his eyes. My dad could not drive for some time because he couldn't see. He would see dark bubbly circles floating around his eyes which kept him from having a clear picture of what was ahead of him. This was another reason why we suggested he stop working and accept dialysis. He was becoming a danger to himself and others on the road if he couldn't see clearly.

I'm surprised my dad doesn't suffer from depression. In 2018, he almost lost his vision, lost one kidney, and had kidney failure. Then he lost his job due to his health issues, he separated from my mom, which eventually led to divorce, not to mention being on the kidney transplant list while suffering every time he went to dialysis.

We were not aware that something went wrong in his arm when they implanted the fistula for dialysis.

My dad complained of pain and numbing during dialysis to the point that his fingers lost sensitivity and feeling. He was told he had to get used to the symptoms because he hadn't gone through that process before but would get better. However, he never did. After his kidney transplant in November 2018, my dad had the fistula removed and found out his arm had damage and would not go back to normal. He was diagnosed with carpal tunnel syndrome and a pinched nerve, for which they did surgery in 2019.

Looking at my dad's life over the past two years, I feel the strong need to invest in my health for myself and my children. I have committed to work out at least 3 times a week and prepare to run a marathon one day soon. As a daughter, I don't want to see my kids in my shoes any time soon and the only way I can help myself is by trying to live a healthier life. I will treat my life like a business in which I am the CEO and have full control. The direction is contingent on my choices. I can invest thirty minutes almost every day to help reduce the possibility of any hereditary illness. No one knows what the future holds for our health, but if I can help delay it or prevent it, I am willing to invest. Are you?

Self-Reflection

Treating my health like a business will help me to possibly live a healthier and longer life. If I only invest thirty minutes a day to help reduce many of the illnesses I mentioned, I think it's worth the risk. Anyone who has a sick family member and is at risk for hereditary illness should also consider this investment.

Am I taking the necessary steps every day to be healthier?

_____

_____

_____

How can I involve my family to improve our health together?

_____

_____

_____

What is my regular diet?

_____

_____

_____

Do I cook healthy meals for my family?

_____

_____

_____

Do I teach my children how to eat healthy?

_____

_____

_____

Chapter Seven:

Every Business Has A Balance

"Ask and it shall be given to you. Seek, and you shall find. Knock, and it shall be opened to you."

-Mathew 7:7

My brother Juan and I were raised in Mexico by my grandfather Cirilo and grandma Hermelinda until I was seven. When my mom moved to Wisconsin, she met my dad and married him and later took me and my brother, but after some time I realized I didn't like it and went back to Mexico for another year. My grandparents were my parents, along with one of my aunts, Olga, who was like a sister to me. She took care of us and helped with our school work. Aunt Olga is the reason I love and believe in God. As a matter of fact, she took me to church the first time. I was about five or six and she gave me gum as a bribe to stay awake during mass. When that didn't work, she would make sure we were standing instead of sitting. She introduced me to our religion, but more importantly, she introduced me to God. Throughout the years I have learned that there is no right or wrong religion, there is only the relationship we have with God; religion has nothing to do with it.

My dad, for example, was raised Catholic. He has never spoken to us about the Bible and doesn't attend church regularly, but he is the first one who gives to the less fortunate. Plus, he follows the ten commandments to the best of his ability and tells us if we live by their example, we will not live a bad life. The teaching brings me to an example I feel is important to mention. I worked with a person who was stealing from our employer every chance she had but was at church every Sunday in the front row.

My aunt Olga has been like my older sister throughout the years. She gives me advice when I need it and now that her daughters Heidi and Yailin are grown, they can also count on me when they need me. I love them as if they were my nieces. I know the baby, Fabiola, loves me as much as I love her. Their brother Diego is the only boy, but he is quiet and prefers keeping to himself.

Since I can remember, my heart has belonged to God, along with reading the Bible to learn more of His teachings. There were times I picked up the Bible and read many scriptures from it but to be honest I have not read it completely. I remember when my sister Mimi was little, I read some of the Bible to her as well. It was important to me that she learned to develop her relationship with Him as I had done.

My faith has kept me moving forward; many times, when I was married to Joe, I would go into the backyard after one of our arguments and ask God *Why me*? I didn't consider myself a bad person. I am not perfect but I know I didn't hurt people for me to feel hurt and live in the situation I was living in.

In the silence after talking with God, I could hear, whether it was me responding to myself or the Holy Spirit responding to comfort me, "Because I know you can."

The reason is moot, I know it was faith. I could handle the situation. One day before I had Angel, one of the arguments was so bad, I tried to commit suicide. I took a bottle of pills to the restroom and swallowed as many as possible. Since I wasn't coming out of the restroom, Joe broke in and made me throw up, then called me stupid for doing what I did. I was tired and he wouldn't let me go home. Joe was right, I was stupid at that moment. I look back now and say to anyone else struggling with this decision, please wait. You can have a bright future. Suicide is not the answer, it is a permanent solution.

At times when you think it should be the end, realize that when it gets the darkest in the tunnel it is because you are about to see the light on the other end.

The Bible says, ask and it will be given, but it also says that God helps those who help themselves. I love these two quotes and feel they go hand in hand. We have to find a balance, 'A Business Called Life.' The way I find a balance is by believing in God. I believed in Him before but didn't understand his love for us until I had my children. As a parent, I know that no matter how good or bad my kids are I love them both the same. If one of them goes astray, I will fight to get them back to where I need them to be. If any of my kids need help, I will be there to help them and guide them no matter what the problem is. If he or she offends and asks forgiveness, I give it to them. I imagine this is the love God has for us. He is our Father and loves us as much as we love our children. He is Almighty and able to help us with anything that we ask, if it's right for us and if the time is right, just like we would for our children. Sometimes we get signs or messages, or even both, to let us know He is listening. But we must learn how to see those signs with an open heart.

For example, when I was pregnant with Angel and having problems with Joe, I had a dream. In my dream, I was in a car accident and my car had flipped upside down. I was on the same street where Joe threatened to kill me and made me beg for my life. The dream showed me a bright light, and I thought it was a train coming to run over my car. But as the light got brighter and I opened my eyes, I saw Jesus Christ floating in the air, slowly approaching me. I saw Him from head to toe. He was wearing very simple sandals made of what appeared to be gold. He had a beautiful white robe with a golden rope wrapped around his waist, His hair was shoulder length and a bit wavy. He had a brighter light around his head, and He approached me holding out his hand.

As soon as He gave me His hand, I closed my eyes. "I don't want to go with you, because I am pregnant."

He shook his head and said, "Jesus."

I replied, "I know you are Jesus; I'm telling you I don't want to go with you yet because I'm pregnant."

One more time, He shook his head. "Jesus." I was getting frustrated; I already knew He was Jesus. He kept approaching with His hand held out.

I didn't give him my hand and for the third time, I said, "I know you are Jesus, but I'm telling you I'm pregnant and don't want to die. I want to see my baby" (I still didn't know the sex of my baby).

His hand got closer to me, and I closed my eyes, as I heard Him say for the third time, "Jesus."

I suddenly woke from my dream; my heart was pounding so hard. The only thing I could move was my eyes. My room was white and for an instant, I thought I was in the hospital. After a few seconds, I realized it was in my room and it was all a dream.

Angel was born on a Good Friday. It was the easiest delivery anyone could ask for. Joe and I arrived at the hospital around 6:30 A.M. and Angel was born at 9:50 A.M, with no epidural and only two pushes. We didn't have a boy name yet since Joe was going to name him if it was a boy. But he had not decided on a name yet either. I wanted to name him Jesus because of my dream, however, I didn't want anyone to think I was crazy. Joe later said we should name him Angel. My mom was in the room, and without knowing about my dream she said we should give him Jesus as his middle name since he was born on Good Friday.

My heart started beating faster and I knew that was a sign. Maybe God wanted me to name my son Jesus? So, Angel's middle name is Jesus and I love it.

The most recent sign from God was when my dad got ill. I used to pray for the best outcome. I would ask God if I could help my dad in any way, please let me help him, but if it was His choice for my dad to go, I was surrendering. *I understand if it is my dad's time to go....*

My mom, sister, my dad's younger brother Antonio and myself signed up to be my dad's kidney donors. I wanted nothing more than to be able to help him, but on the other hand, I was scared of not being able to help. My mom couldn't donate because she had high blood pressure. My sister Mimi was told she had to lose weight. My uncle was not yet tested and then it was me. Unfortunately, my dad, Jorge is not my biological dad, and to be a donor we had to have the same blood type. Many people do not know my dad is not my biological dad because we have loved each other like if I was. I was mortified, thinking since I wasn't his biological daughter, that the chance of me being a match to him was very slim. I started working out and trying to be healthy just in case our blood type did match. I didn't want to have a reason not to donate if I was a match to his blood type. To be a donor you have to be healthy, with no signs of diabetes, high blood pressure, or any other illness that affects the kidneys.

The time finally came when the insurance approved all the tests. To my surprise, my dad and I did have the same blood type. I was relieved!! I hadn't told my dad yet that I was testing. The next step was getting tested for diabetes and antibodies. They had to make sure I was not diabetic and my dad's antibodies were not going to fight my kidney. I passed that test also! Then I had to go to Baylor in Dallas and make sure my heart and all my other organs were healthy enough for surgery and make sure my one kidney was healthy enough to do the work of two.

I finally received a call from Baylor saying I was healthy enough and a perfect match for my dad!! I knew God had helped me. I mean, I am not my dad's biological daughter but was his perfect match. So, if you're wondering how my dad was only on dialysis for a few months and survived, I am the answer.

We applied, got tested, and moved quickly to get the transplant done as soon as possible. The last thing I wanted to do was lose my father after God blessed our lives with a miracle.

I finally told my dad once everything was approved and had scheduled a date for surgery. I decided to write a letter, explaining how I felt. I told him how thankful I was that he married my mom and adopted me and my other brother Juan. I thanked him for always treating me like a biological daughter and for never making me feel any less. I told him I'd rather live without a kidney than without my dad. We all cried, and at first, he didn't want to accept my help, but he later understood that God had given us this opportunity. I was going to live a long life, providing I took care of myself.

My dad and I had the surgery at Baylor Dallas in November of 2018. A few months later, his doctor stopped the high blood pressure medicine my dad had been taking and lowered his insulin. His kidney was working perfectly. It was a miracle that could only have been provided by God.

"I ask God for good health; I ask him for work because if I have work, I can help those around me. I ask him for patience and guidance. I love the prayer Our Father."

The prayer above is one of the best I have found. In it we pray for bountiful blessings, forgiveness affirming, and forgive those who trespass against us.

A Business Called Life is more than just the title of this book, it is a message that I wanted to pass along. We must learn to find balance between life and the pressures of society.

Self-Reflection

What have I learned by reading *A Business Called Life*?

_____

_____

_____

How can I use these methods to improve my life?

_____

_____

_____

What are my goals for the future?

_____

_____

_____

Make a list of goals to accomplish this year.

_____

_____

_____

Epilogue

The ability to move forward, forgiving the people that have hurt you, is more about helping you than them. By forgiving someone, it allows you to find peace within yourself. For example, I forgave Joe. I have not forgotten his actions; it has made me stronger. I don't wish him bad, on the contrary, I wish him well and hope he learned how not to treat a woman. I want him to be happy; far from me and my family, but happy. That one simple action is how you find balance in life. The balance is what brings happiness.